Brontë COUNTRY

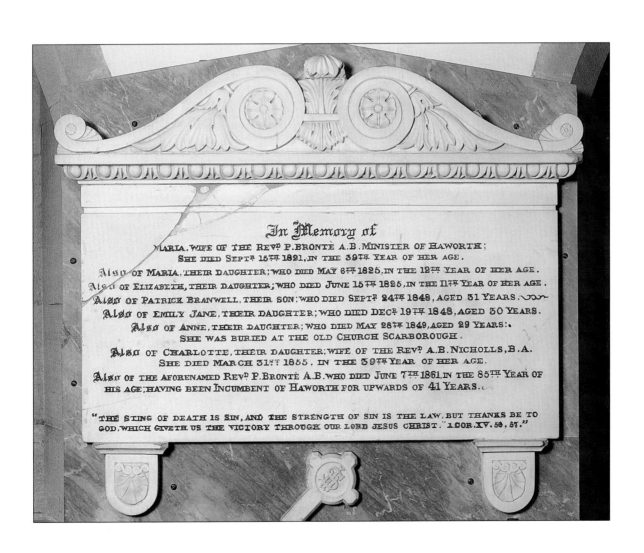

Brontë COUNTRY

Tom Howard

SMITHMARK

AM BT JC LK CADCC RH CS

PHOTOGRAPHIC ACKNOWLEDGEMENTS
Jacket front cover main picture:
Fortean Picture Library
Jacket front cover colour insets:
Comstock Photo Library
Jacket front cover black and white insets:
Hulton Deutsch Collection
Jacket back cover
Comstock Photo Library

Inside pages
By Courtesy of The National Portrait Gallery, London
6.

Comstock Photo Library
12, 17 top, 21, 45 bottom, 63 top, bottom
(Simon McBride) 10, 11 both, 13, 16 left, 24 top, bottom, 25 top, 26 top,
bottom, 30 top, bottom, 35 top, bottom, 38 bottom, 40, 41, 42-43, 46-47,
54, 65 top, bottom, 67, 69 top, 70 top, bottom, 74 bottom, 76, 77 top, bottom, 78, 79 top, bottom.

Derek Forss Photography
16 right, 18, 48-49, 53.

Simon Warner
1, 2-3, 4-5, 14, 15, 17 bottom, 19, 20, 23, 25 bottom, 27, 28, 31, 32,
36-37, 38-39, 45 top, 49, 50, 56-57, 58, 59, 60, 62, 64, 66, 68, 69 bottom, 71, 72-73, 74 top, 80.

Map: Malcolm Porter

Page 1: The Brontë Memorial Plaque in Haworth Church
Pages 2-3: Haworth Moor
These pages: The Worth Valley from Penistone Hill

This edition first published in the United States in 1995 by SMITHMARK
Publishers Inc., 16 East 32nd Street, New York, NY 10016.

SMITHMARK books are available for bulk purchase for sales promotion and
premium use. For details write or call the manager of special sales,
SMITHMARK Publishers, 16 East 32nd Street, New York, NY 10016;
(212) 532 6600.

Produced by: Regency House Publishing Limited
The Grange, Grange Yard, London, SE1 3AG.

ISBN 0-8317-1855-2

Printed in the U.A.E.

10 9 8 7 6 5 4 3 2 1

CONTENTS

INTRODUCTION 6

THE EARLY DAYS 10

GROWING UP AT HAWORTH 22

PUPILS AND TEACHERS 34

A SCHOOL OF THEIR OWN? 51

PUBLICATION 56

FAME AND MRS. NICHOLLS 72

998

INTRODUCTION

The three Brontë sisters, Charlotte, Emily and Anne, were together an exceptional phenomenon. For a family to produce one writer of international renown is unusual, but three in a single generation is a remarkable achievement. There may have been many other early-Victorian young ladies who, along with the needlework, watercolours and improving reading with which they occupied their leisure time, wrote verse

The Brontë sisters, painted by their brother Branwell c. 1825. Left to right are Anne, Emily and Charlotte. The figure painted out in the centre may have been a self-portrait of the artist.

or stories for their own amusement or for private circulation among family and close friends. Some even achieved publication. These three Yorkshire women, however, showed unusual narrative skill and literary talent.

Drawing upon their personal experiences and close observation of the world around them, they combined powerful imaginative skills to produce novels which have become acknowledged classics. A century-and-a-half after they were originally published they are still immensely popular and widely read. They have brought pleasure to further millions through theatre, film and television adaptations which have brought characters such as Heathcliffe, Catherine Earnshaw, Mr. Rochester and Jane Eyre vividly to stage and screen. Between them, the Brontë sisters produced only seven novels, but these have won for them a unique and lasting place in the annals of literature and in the hearts of their readers.

The Brontës were by no means instant successes as poets and novelists. Publishing at first under pseudonyms, partly to avoid a presumed prejudice against female novelists and partly to preserve their anonymity, their first book of poems sold only two copies. Charlotte's *The Professor* was at first rejected by the publisher to whom she sent it, but the same company took *Jane Eyre*, which had an immediate success, much more than that of her sisters' *Wuthering Heights* and *Agnes Grey* which followed the same year.

The Brontë's own story has exerted as strong a fascination as the contents of their books. Their short lives centred on their family home, a parsonage in a village set in a cleft of the Yorkshire Moors, which has since become a place of pilgrimage for many thousands of admirers every year. The streets of Haworth are now known to people from all over the globe who may also, perhaps, take home a memory of the wildness and beauty of the surrounding countryside.

The details of the Brontë family's lives first became known following the publication of a biography of Charlotte by Mrs. Gaskell in 1857, only two years after Charlotte's death. Elizabeth Gaskell was herself already an acclaimed novelist, much admired by Charlotte, who was delighted to become her friend after they met in 1850. The furore which this book caused, not least because of its allegedly libellous statements which caused them to be withdrawn, contributed greatly to the establishment of the Brontës' posthumous fame and encouraged interest in their own history because of its close connections with their fictional creations as objects of public interest. A great many books since have investigated their story further.

The nature of the sisters' lives and those of their characters is deeply rooted in the circumstances and the locations in which they lived, as is immediately recognizable by those who are able to visit them. The places which form the settings in their novels may have been given different names, but they often bear a close relation to places well-known to them, sometimes containing characteristics drawn from several different locations. This book seeks to present some of that topographical background and to relate it to the Brontës' lives and works. It will be an evocative reminder for those who have personally explored these locations, and an armchair guide for those who cannot see them for themselves at first hand.

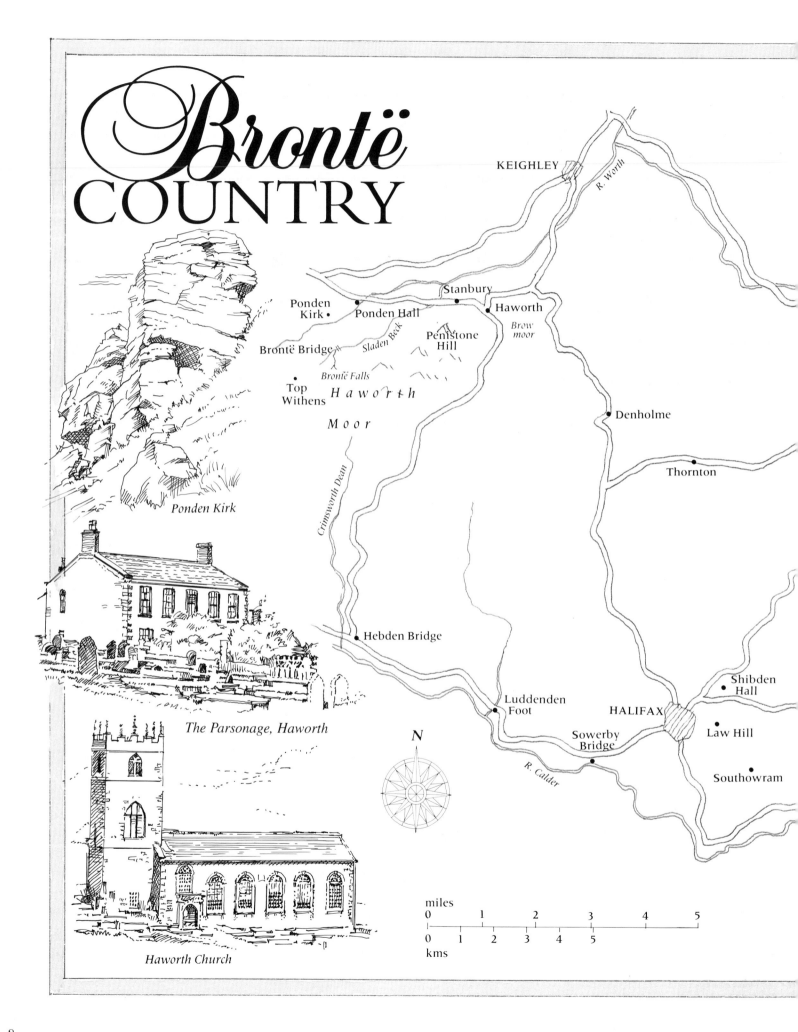

Brontë COUNTRY

KEIGHLEY

R. Worth

Stanbury

Ponden
Kirk

Ponden Hall

Haworth

*Brow
moor*

Brontë Bridge

Sladen Beck

Penistone
Hill

Brontë Falls

Top
Withens

H a w o r t h

Denholme

M o o r

Thornton

Grimsworth Dean

Ponden Kirk

Hebden Bridge

Shibden
Hall

The Parsonage, Haworth

Luddenden
Foot

HALIFAX

Law Hill

N

Sowerby
Bridge

Southowram

R. Calder

miles

| 0 | | 1 | | 2 | | 3 | | 4 | | 5 |

| 0 | 1 | 2 | 3 | 4 | 5 |

kms

Haworth Church

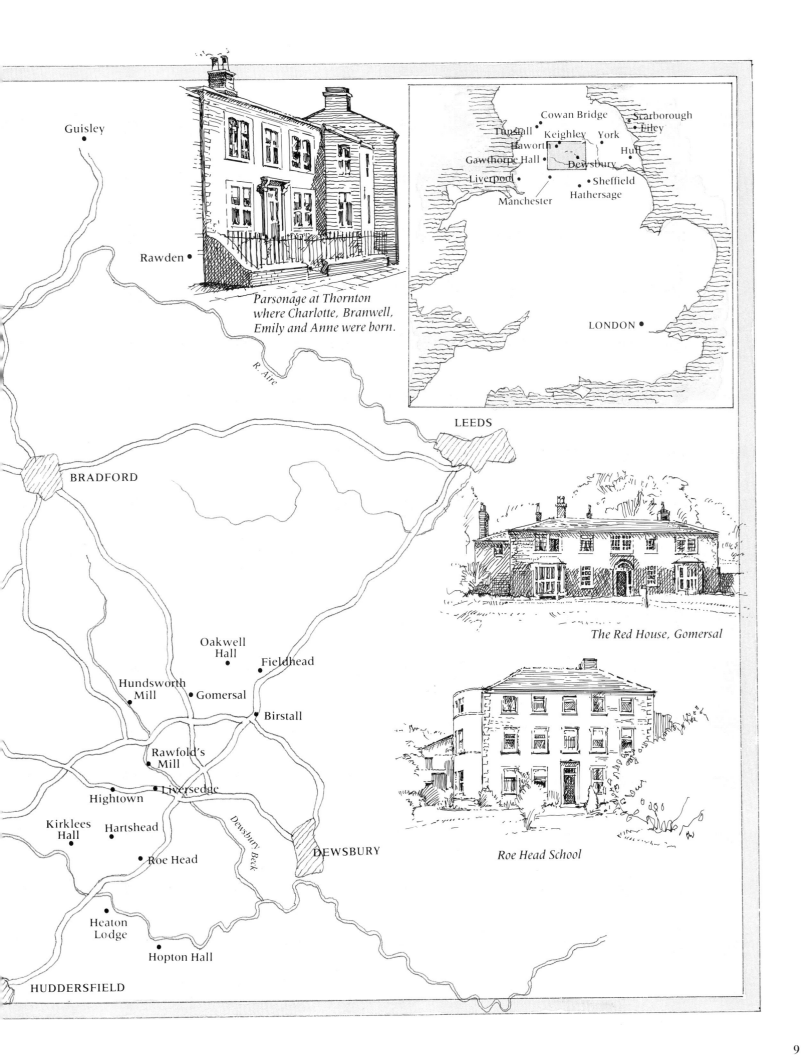

Parsonage at Thornton where Charlotte, Branwell, Emily and Anne were born.

Cowan Bridge
Scarborough
Tunstall
Filey
Keighley
York
Haworth
Hull
Gawthorpe Hall
Dewsbury
Liverpool
Sheffield
Manchester
Hathersage

LONDON

LEEDS

Guisley

Rawden

R. Aire

BRADFORD

Oakwell Hall

Fieldhead

Hundsworth Mill

Gomersal

Birstall

Rawfold's Mill

Liversedge

Hightown

Kirklees Hall

Hartshead

Roe Head

Dewsbury Beck

DEWSBURY

Heaton Lodge

Hopton Hall

HUDDERSFIELD

The Red House, Gomersal

Roe Head School

EARLY DAYS

Woodhouse Grove School, Apperley Bridge, near Bradford, where Patrick Brontë examined the boys in religious instruction and where he first met his wife Maria.

The Brontës were not a Yorkshire family. The parents were of Irish and Cornish descent – indeed, in her teens Charlotte is said still to have had an Irish accent. Their father, Patrick, was born in 1777, son of an Irish peasant, in the village of Drumballyroney which nestles in the foothills of the Mountains of Mourne. His family name was more usually written as Brunty (or Branty or even Prunty). He taught himself to read and, after being apprenticed to a blacksmith, then working as a linen weaver, he got a job teaching in a local village school. When he was not much more than 16, the vicar of nearby Drumgooland engaged him as tutor to his two sons.

His employer, the Reverend Thomas Tighe, a friend of preacher John Wesley, saw potential in young Patrick who, with his help, obtained a place at St. John's College, Cambridge. He was 25-years-old when, apart from the sea crossing, he walked all the way to Cambridge to take up his place as an exhibitioner. The award required him to coach others and perform various menial tasks for his place and college assistance. It was supplemented by a grant from the Church Missionary Society.

His name in the St. Johns' College records is entered successively as Brants, Bronte, Bronté and finally Brontë – accented like that of the Duke of Brontë, the already famous Admiral Horatio Nelson. That was the name under which he was awarded his Bachelor of Arts degree in 1806 and

was subsequently ordained as a clergyman in the Church of England.

After brief spells in Essex and Shropshire, he became curate at the woollen mill-town of Dewsbury, thus bringing him to Yorkshire. In 1811, he obtained the living of the parish of St. Peter in the village of Hartshead, not far from Dewsbury and overlooking the valley of the River Calder.

William Morgan, a friend who had been a fellow curate in Shropshire, was engaged to marry the daughter of the headmaster of a boarding school ten miles away at Woodhouse Grove, Apperley Bridge, near Bradford. He took Patrick Brontë to meet the Fennel family who found he shared their evangelical enthusiasms and invited him to become examiner in Bible studies to the school.

There, Patrick met the Fennel's niece, Maria Branwell, an assistant at the school, and a deep affection developed between the two. At the end of December, less than five months after their first meeting, they were married in a double wedding beside her cousin and William Morgan at nearby St. Oswald's, Guiseley. The men each conducted the other's ceremony and the women were bridesmaids to each other.

Maria, daughter of a prosperous merchant family, had been left a modest private income on the death of her parents. She was 29, Patrick 35. They set up house in Clough Lane, Hightown where two daughters were born: Maria in January 1813, Elizabeth in February 1815. Later that year Patrick

Haworth viewed from the hills above. The village is still much the same size as it was when the Brontës lived there. This is the sort of prospect they would have seen when returning from walks upon the moors.

exchanged his living for one at Thornton, near Bradford, There, four more children were born: Charlotte in 1816, Branwell in 1817, Emily in 1818 and Anne in 1820.

Children were not their only creation. Both parents tried their hand at literary composition. Before their mar-

riage, Patrick had issued a volume of *Cottage Poems* through a printer in Halifax. These were intentionally simple, clearly expressed verses aimed at an untutored readership, a book for slow readers to help them improve their literacy. More poems followed with *The Rural Minstrel*, in 1813, a moral tale,

at Haworth.

St. Michael's Church at Haworth had been established centuries before as a 'chapel of ease' for those who could not get to Bradford for services. Officially the post was that of 'perpetual curate', not vicar, but although technically subordinate to the Vicar of Bradford, it involved similar responsibilities in the parish. Patrick Brontë was to remain there for more than four decades, though the next year he became a widower, and his children motherless, when Maria died of cancer in September 1821.

Mrs. Brontë's sister, Elizabeth Branwell, had come to Haworth to help nurse Maria in her last illness. She was able to stay to look after the children for the time being – the eldest was only seven and they were themselves ill with

Haworth from the quarry above the village, which gave employment to some of its menfolk. The tower of St. Michael's stands above most of the houses.

The Cottage in the Woods, in 1815 (which went into three editions), and a novel, *The Maid of Killarney, or Albion and Flora*, published anonymously in London in 1818.

In February 1820, only a month after Anne's birth, they moved again, to the Glebe House (now the Parsonage)

scarlet fever when their mother died. But who was to care for his home and family in future? The Reverend Brontë considered the possibility of remarriage and proposed to Elizabeth Firth, a friend in Thornton who was little Anne's godmother. She turned him down. So, in 1823, did Mary

The church of St. Michael and All Angels, Haworth. The building was considerably altered after the Brontës' time. The tower was raised by the extra courses which accommodate the clock and the body of the church was replaced by a new nave and aisles in the Gothic Revival style so popular with Victorian church architects and restorers.

OPPOSITE
Looking down the main street of Haworth. Many of Haworth's streets retain their old cobbled surfaces.

The approach to Haworth and The Parsonage.

'For a short distance the road appears to turn away from Haworth, as it winds round the base of the shoulder of a hill, but then it crosses a bridge over the "beck", and the ascent through the village begins. The flag-stones with which it is paved are placed end-ways, in order to give a better hold to the horses' feet; and, even with this help, they seem to be in constant danger of slipping backwards. The old stone houses are high compared to the width of the street, which makes an abrupt turn before reaching the more level ground at the head of the village, so that the steep aspect of the place, in one part, is almost like that of a wall. But this surmounted, the church lies a little off the main road on the left; a hundred yards, or so, and the driver relaxes his care, and the horse breathes more easily, as they pass into the quiet little by-street that leads to Haworth Parsonage. The churchyard is to one side of this lane, the school-house and the sexton's dwelling on the other. The parsonage stands at right angles to the road, facing down upon the church; so that, in fact, parsonage, church and belfried schoolhouse, form three sides of an irregular oblong, of which the fourth is open to the fields and moors that lie beyond. The area of this oblong is filled up by a crowded churchyard, and a small garden or court in front of the clergyman's house. As the entrance to this from the road is at the side, the path goes round the corner into the little plot of ground. Underneath the windows is a narrow flower-border, carefully tended in days of yore, although only the most hardy plants could be made to grow there. Within the stone wall, which keeps out the surrounding churchyard, are bushes of elder and lilac; the rest of the ground is occupied by a square grass plot and a gravel walk. The house is of grey stone, two stories high, heavily roofed with flags, in order to resist the winds that might strip off a lighter covering.'

From *The Life of Charlotte Brontë* by Mrs Gaskell

15

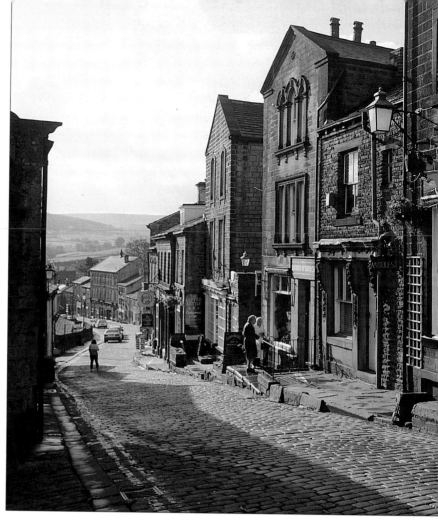

The streets and alleyways of Haworth. From almost everywhere in the village the surrounding hills are visible, except upon those days when the mists close in or a snowstorm fills the view.

Burder, to whom he had become briefly engaged when a curate in Wethersfield in Essex. She responded (though with a rather more polite turn of phrase) to the effect that she felt she had been lucky to escape him last time and certainly refused to be prevailed upon now. Eventually, Aunt Elizabeth was persuaded to make Glebe House her permanent home and to assume responsibility for the care of the children and the running of the household.

The Reverend Brontë has sometimes been presented as the archetypal Victorian paterfamilias, stern, forbidding and repressive but, in fact, children seemed to like him very much and he certainly had a fondness for small children and their 'amusing ways'. He encouraged his own to read widely and to join in discussions of political and public news, literature and the arts.

Aunt Branwell also followed this example, encouraging them to become well informed and able to express their own ideas and opinions. The children show little sign of affection for her in their surviving letters and it is likely that she lacked the outgoing warm personality of their mother. But she ran the house conscientiously, however much she adversely compared Haworth with Penzance: the need to respect their maiden aunt's privacy may have added to the sense of independence which developed among the children of the family.

At Haworth, their father supervised the education of the eldest, but Aunt Branwell was the children's main teacher. At lessons in her room they were taught to read and write and the girls learned needlework. Some of the samplers they stitched can still be seen in the Parsonage Museum; but the emphasis was not on the decorative embroideries which the daughters of the wealthy would have learned as a suitable feminine accomplishment, but rather on practical sewing: this would

have included repairs and turning cuffs and collars to extend a garment's life.

Aunt Branwell kept household help in the persons of young Nancy and Sarah Garrs, but the girls would have been expected to lend a hand with chores and so learn the rudiments of good housekeeping. Aunt Branwell had her own small means and with an income of about £200 a year Patrick Brontë was no pauper – even a century later many a working man would have been glad to earn as much – and the parsonage came rent-free. He had come a long way from his peasant background and there were now different expectations for the family of a clergyman. However, there was little to spare to pay for the education of six children, to equip them to make their own way in the world.

The two eldest girls did, for a short time, attend a school at Crofton, near Wakefield, but were withdrawn, perhaps because of the expense. However,

17

The Parsonage at Haworth. The gabled portion to the right was added in the second half of the 19th century, after Patrick Brontë's death, but the body of the house is much as it was when Brontë lived here.

in 1824, the establishment of the Clergy Daughters' School as a semi-charitable institution appeared to solve the immediate problem. Subsidized by charitable donations, its charge forboard and instruction was a nominal fee of only £14 per annum. It was planned to link the school with a senior establishment which would offer further training as governesses, offering a clergyman 'a two-fold advantage of a sound and cheap education, and future provision for his daughters.'

The school was about 50 miles (80km) from Haworth, at Cowan Bridge, on the borders of Westmoreland and Lancashire. There Mr. Brontë took eleven-year-old Maria and nine-year-old Elizabeth to join its first group of pupils in July 1824 – measles and whooping cough had prevented them from starting earlier in the year. He made the journey again in August with Charlotte (aged eight) and in November with Emily (only six), the youngest of all the pupils at the school.

The school records show that, when they arrived, little Emily read 'very prettily', that Charlotte was 'altogether clever of her age, but knows nothing systematically', Elizabeth 'reads a little, writes pretty well ... works very badly

the school was especially cold in winter. The founder, wealthy evangelist and writer of improving stories for children, William Carus Wilson, himself ordered the provisions and was anxious to ensure their good quality but, as Mrs. Gaskell, who talked to those who had been at school with the Brontës recounts:

'... the cook, who had much of his confidence, and against whom for a long time no one durst utter complaint, was careless, dirty and wasteful. To some children, oatmeal porridge is distasteful, and consequently un-wholesome, even when properly made; at Cowan Bridge School it was often sent up, not merely burnt, but with offensive fragments of other substances discovered in it. The beef, that should hae been carefully salted before it was dressed, had often become tainted from neglect; and the house seemed to be pervaded, morning, noon, and night, by the odour of rancid fat that had steamed out of the oven in which much of their food was prepared.'

Cooking was often done with water contaminated with dirt from the roof, milk tainted by dirty pans and on

Cottages at Cowan Bridge. Set back some distance from the banks of the River Leck, they housed Cowan Bridge School, to which the older Brontë girls were sent. The surviving buildings housed the dining-room, staff bedrooms and the lodgings of the superintendant. Carus Wilson added a wing at right-angles at one end of these cottages as classrooms and dormitories and at the other a covered veranda for taking exercise in bad weather. The additions were destroyed in a fire after the school closed and the remainder reverted to being private cottages.

and knows nothing else', while Maria read tolerably, wrote pretty well, knew a little grammar, geography and history and could read a little French but knew no French grammar and was bad at needlework. The school did not judge highly what education their father and Aunt Branwell had instilled. The teachers would have been even more critical of their liberal upbringing, for Cowan Bridge was strict and authoritarian, founded on a strong belief in corrective discipline in order to subdue the inherent wickedness of children.

To strict discipline was added poorly-prepared food and discomfort:

Tunstall Church, where the Brontë girls attended service each Sunday when they were at Cowan Bridge School. It is fictionalized as Brocklebridge.

Saturdays, a pie was served made up from scraps collected all week in the dirty larder.

On Sundays the pupils walked well over 2 miles (more then 3km) across country to Tunstall to hear their founder preach at morning and after-noon services at the parish church.

Since it was too far to go back for their midday meal they took a cold dinner with them and, according to Mrs. Gaskell, 'ate it in a chamber over the entrance opening out of one of the former galleries.' Cold, and with their feet soaked from tramping through the snow or across muddy fields, they were forced to remain all day in the unheated church.

Charlotte's own account of Cowan Bridge can be found in fictional form as Lowood in *Jane Eyre*, its horrors confirmed by Mrs. Gaskell's research, though there were threats of libel actions from those associated with the running of the school.

Winter brought sickness. Maria, even worse treated by one of the insensitive mistresses than her fictional counterpoint, little Helen Burns in *Jane Eyre*, went down with 'low fever' and was sent home in February 1825. She died at Haworth in early May. Meanwhile, Elizabeth was ill with tuberculosis and was forced to return home at the end of the month. Anxious for his other daughters, Reverend Brontë set off to fetch them too. When he arrived at Cowan Bridge he found they were not there but had been sent to Mr. Wilson's seaside house at Silverdale. From there he brought them home to Haworth where Elizabeth died on 15 June. He was determined that his remaining daughters would not be returning to Cowan Bridge.

For the time being at least, Charlotte, Emily and Anne would be taught at home. Branwell too, who may have for a short time attended a local school, was instructed by his father when time could be spared from parish duties. The Reverend Brontë, B.A. (Cantab) was better qualified than the local pedagogues and tutored his son in Latin and Greek as well as the three Rs.

There had been another, happier change at the Parsonage at the beginning of the year. Tabitha Aykroyd arrived, to replace the Garrs sisters who had left. She was to be cook and general domestic there for 30 years, joined later by Martha Brown, one of the parish sexton's daughters who started off in service at the age of ten and left only to accompany Charlotte's widower to Ireland. Tabitha was a Yorkshirewoman of 54, a widow who had only just returned to the district after working on a farm. She was there to nurse Maria and Elizabeth in their final days. Tabby became a great friend to the children and was greatly loved by them. Later she was probably the model for Nelly Dean, the narrator of much of *Wuthering Heights*, and may have provided material for parts of that story, in tales of strange past events in the Haworth neighbourhood.

Each Sunday, the pupils of Cowan Bridge school walked across the fields to reach Tunstall Church.

'During January, February, and part of March, the deep snows, and after their melting, the almost impassable roads, prevent our stirring beyond the garden walls, except to go to church

'Sundays were dreary days in that winter season. We had to walk two miles to Brocklebridge Church ... We set out cold, we arrived at church colder; during the morning service we became almost paralyzed. It was too far to return to dinner, and an allowance of cold meat and bread, in the same proportion observed in our ordinary meals, was served round between services.

'At the close of the afternoon service we returned by an exposed and hilly road, where the bitter wind, blowing over a range of snowy summits to the north, almost flayed the skin from our faces.'

Jane Eyre Chapter 7

GROWING UP AT HAWORTH

The loss of his two elder daughters seemed to distance Patrick Brontë from his other children, who became ever more dependent upon one another, for they had few opportunities for close contact with other playmates. The Parsonage children had little in common with Haworth children of the same age who were already at work in the Yorkshire woollen industry. Tabby Aykroyd, however, did form a very definite link with Haworth and its people and became an important part of their lives. In warm and affectionate contrast to the more austere Aunt Branwell, she gave to and gained from them an unquestioning affection. With her forthright Yorkshire commonsense and practical influence, she managed to curb, to a certain extent, the wilder flights of the Brontë children's imagination.

That imagination found its greatest outlet in the fantasy lands which they created in an outpouring of juvenile literary activity which far exceeds their adult output. A little 16-page book still survives, which Charlotte wrote for her sister Anne, dating from as early as 1824. In just 125 words, it tells the story of another little girl called Anne. Another survival is a miniature book in which Branwell recorded and illustrated the exploits of his toy soldiers. The Reverend Brontë later told Mrs. Gaskell that as soon as the children could read and write they 'used to invent and act little plays of their own.'

The creation of their fantasy worlds seems to have been sparked into existence by some gifts brought back by their father from a trip to Leeds in 1826. These included a set of ninepins, a toy village and a box of wooden soldiers for Branwell to augment his depleted army. The children had already gone to bed when their father arrived home but Branwell recorded discovering the soldiers by his bed next morning and how he took them in to his sisters and gave them one each to name and look after. As an extension to the games which these toys inspired, it was decided that their imaginary lives, speeches and exploits should be recorded in journals and books as though they were real people. The children began to create miniature books and magazines which closely followed those they already knew, such as Branwell's *The Young Men's Magazine* in imitation of *Blackwood's Magazine*, complete with correspondence column.

At first, each of the soldiers had an imaginary kingdom of his own, but these were eventually amalgamated to form the 'Great Glass Town Confederacy', for which Branwell redrew part of the map of Africa with twelve kingdoms for the twelve soldiers. Glasstown had its own history and was complete with celebrities and scoundrels, its presiding rulers (the Four Genii), generals, heroes, artists, tradespeople, writers, publishers and printers.

Many children make up their own books and magazines – this was even more natural in a household where books in their father's library included some with his own name on the title page – but for them this was no passing

Mrs. Gaskell described Haworth Parsonage as she saw it in the 1850s in her *Life of Charlotte Brontë*:

'It appears to have been built about a hundred years ago, and to consist of four rooms on each story; the two windows on the right (as the visitor stands, with his back to the church, ready to enter at the front door) belonging to Mr. Brontë's study, the two on the left to the family sitting room. Everything about the place tells of the most dainty order, the most exquisite cleanliness. The door-steps are spotless; the small old-fashioned window-panes glitter like looking-glass.

Inside and outside of that house cleanliness goes up into its essence, purity.'

That cleanliness was the more impressive given the standards of Haworth hygiene a century and a half ago. The Parsonage itself had no modern sanitation – only a double-seater privy in the backyard that was used by the whole family and their servants. In the village, provision was much less. An inspector's report of 1850 listed two privies open to public view in the street, shared by a dozen families, and another had a cesspit below that which was cleared through a small door onto the street which was often burst open by the pressure of unremoved night-soil. Animals were kept close to living quarters. Charcoal stoves burned day and night to keep the temperature right for working the wool in unventilated and overcrowded houses, and water supplies were poor and could give out in the summer months when epidemics of typhus were prevalent. Forty per cent of children died before reaching the age of six.

Charlotte herself believed that the parsonage was built over an old part of the graveyard and the well which supplied their drinking water was sunk through the burials. There was plenty of fresh air on the moors, but conditions in Haworth encouraged disease and infection.

The stone floors were so cold that Aunt Branwell wore wooden pattens to keep her feet off them.

enthusiasm. The output was prodigious and was to continue over many years.

The books themselves are minuscule creations, usually about 2in x 1½in (50mm x 38mm), packed with tiny writing. They have proper title pages and are stitched together, with thicker sugar-bag paper or other shop wrapping for covers. Writing in such a microscopic hand, almost too small to read, and using a quill pen, must have demanded considerable skill, not always matched by their sometimes erratic spelling. These 'publications' must have consumed a great deal of time, yet they were kept a secret between the children.

After 1830, Glasstown was renamed Verreopolis, and then Verdopolis. Branwell and Charlotte invented the kingdom of Angria, the King and Duke of Zamorna was Arthur, imaginary son of the Duke of Wellington for whom one of their soldiers had been named.

FAR LEFT
Mr. Brontë's study. Over the mantlepiece is an engraving of one of John Martin's paintings. His grandiose and dramatic biblical pictures strongly influenced the imaginations of the young Brontës in developing their fantasy lands and making illustrations of them.

LEFT
The Kitchen

LEFT
Brontë Parsonage and Sunday School, Haworth.

FAR LEFT
The dining- and sitting-room of the parsonage. The settee is believed to be that on which Charlotte died. Her writing desk is the table. Ellen Nussey described the house in her *Reminiscences*:

'There was not much carpet anywhere except in the sitting room, and on the study floor. The hall floor and stairs were done with sand-stone, always beautifully clean ... the walls were not papered, but stained in a pretty dove-coloured tint; hair-seated chairs and mahogany tables, bookshelves in the study, but not many of these else-where. Scant and bare indeed, many will say, yet it was not a scantness that made itself felt.'

ABOVE AND OPPOSITE
The 'Brontë Bridge' on a tributary to
South Dean Beck.

RIGHT
'The Brontë Chair', a seat-shaped
rock on Haworth Moor that the
Brontës may well have used to rest on
when tired from walking.

Looking east across Haworth Moor. Charlotte wrote in a letter to James Taylor in 1850:

'My sister Emily had a particular love for [the moors], and there is not a knoll of heather, not a branch of fern, not a young bilberry leaf, not a fluttering lark or linnet, but reminds me of her. The distant prospects were Anne's delight, and when I look round she is in the blue tints, the pale mists, the waves and shadows of the horizon. In the hill-country silence their poetry comes by lines and stanzas into my mind: once I loved it; now I dare not read it ...

Charlotte gave him two wives and several mistresses. Emily and Anne even invented a kingdom of their own, called Gondal, though none of the Gondal books survive, only some of Emily's poems with Gondal subjects. At about the time of his 13th birthday, Branwell's verse included a two-act drama in blank verse on the subject of the Ancient British general Caractacus.

The family's writing was full of humour, and consisted not only of paro-dies of other publications and current events but of satires on one another: Charlotte invented Patrick Benjamin Wiggins as an Angrian caricature of her brother and elsewhere made fun of his enthusiasm for *Ossian* and his poetic and artistic aspirations.

Contemporary attitudes made it much easier for Branwell to take part in Haworth activities than was possible for his sisters. He took a keen interest in the local boxing club and soon made a circle of acquaintance at the Black Bull Inn, including the family of his father's sexton, John Brown. But Charlotte was his favourite companion and she loved him dearly.

Patrick Brontë was possibly always something of a hypochondriac but in the winter of 1830-31 he became seriously sick with a congestion of the lungs, making him all the more concerned for his children's future prospects. If he were to die they would lose their home, which went with the curacy, and he had insufficient means to provide for them. Education away from home was again considered and, with help from her god-parents, Charlotte was enrolled at Roe Head School. This was another relatively new establishment, less than 20 miles (30km) away and about 5 miles (7.5km) from Huddersfield on the turn-pike road to Leeds.

The footpath from Haworth village to the moors passes beneath this avenue of trees.

Sheep on Haworth Moor. Many of Haworth's inhabitants found employment in the rock quarries on Browmore, but wool was at the heart of the Yorkshire economy. Haworth was on a turnpike road and was connected by a web of packhorse trails with the great sheep farming areas of North Yorkshire and Lancashire. Wool was brought to Haworth for combing and weaving and local workers handled more wool than the combers in the town of Bradford. Most of the trade passed through Halifax where a special room was set aside in the wool exchange for Haworth. The quality of Haworth work was so high that it continued even after the introduction of machine processing, the advent of which forms part of the background to Charlotte Brontë's *Shirley*.

The view from Crow Hill. One day Emily, Branwell and Anne were walking on the moors with the Garrs sisters when this part of the moors called Crow Hill which was already a quaking bog, shaking to the tread and with oozing springs and nearby marshes, suddenly erupted. They had taken shelter from a violent thunderstorm when their father, watching it from the parsonage and increasingly concerned for them, heard a distant explosion, quite different from the thunder, and felt a tremor pass through the house.

He preached a sermon about the event, wrote an account for *The Leeds Mercury* and published a pamphlet describing in verse *The Phenomenon ... of the Extraordinary Disruption of a Bog, Which took place in the Moors of Haworth* in the introduction to which he wrote:

'During the time of a tremendous storm of thunder, lightning, and rain, a part of the moors ... sunk into two wide cavities; the larger of which measured three hundred yards in length, above two hundred in breadth, and was five or six yards deep. From these cavities ran deep rivers, which uniting at the distance of a hundred yards, formed a vast volume of mud and water, varying from thirty to sixty yards in breadth, and from five to six in depth; uprooting trees, damaging, or altogether overthrowing solid stone bridges, stopping mills, and occasionally overwhelming fields of corn, all along its course of ten or fifteen miles.'

Scar Hill, a characteristic part of Haworth Moor, with dry-stone walls and coarse windswept grass. The Brontë children all had a deep feeling for their local landscape. In her *Reminiscences* Ellen Nussey wrote that what they

'cared for and lived in most were the surroundings of nature, the free expanse of hill and mountain, the purple heather, the dells, and glens, and brooks, the broad sky view, the whistling winds, the snowy expanse, the starry heavens ...'

PUPILS AND TEACHERS

Although some 20 miles distant, Roe Head was much closer to Haworth than the school at Cowan Bridge. On one occasion Branwell, missing Charlotte's company, walked all the way there and back to see his sister. It was different from the previous establishment in almost every way, with only ten pupils when 14-year-old Charlotte was enrolled, and much more comfortable. Another pupil, Ellen Nussey, who was to become Charlotte's close friend, described the headmistress, Miss Margaret Wooler, as being 'like a lady abbess. She wore white, well-fitting dresses embroidered. Her long hair plaited, formed a coronet, and long large ringlets fell from her head to shoulders. She was not pretty or handsome, but her quiet dignity made her presence imposing. She was nobly scrupulous and conscientious – a woman of the greatest self-denial.'

On arrival, Charlotte gave the impression of having little conventional learning, as the school understood it, and she was placed in a junior class. At first she was utterly miserable and Ellen Nussey found her 'a silent, weeping, dark little figure in the large bay window' of the schoolroom. But her keen intelligence and extensive understanding of certain subjects was soon recognized, despite the shortfall in more conventional knowledge and it was not long before she was winning prizes for her schoolwork and medals for good conduct.

Charlotte was poorly-off compared to her fellow pupils, as was noticeable from her worn, old-fashioned clothes. She remained delicate when fully-grown, and very short-sighted, so that she could never join in ball games and, since at this time she refused to wear her spectacles, was obliged to hold her books within inches of her nose in order to read them.

Charlotte's new friend Ellen belonged to a wealthy, religious and conservative county family (though they were going through temporary financial difficulties following the death of Ellen's father). Mary Taylor, another girl who befriended her soon after her arrival, came from a family of very different background. Although the Taylors went back centuries, and lived in a fine 17th-century house, her father was a cloth manufacturer and they followed a radical, dissenting tradition rather than the Established Anglican Church. Mrs. Taylor was a strict Calvinist, though her children argued incessantly about culture and politics. Mary's tomboyish sister Martha was at Roe Head too. These girls had very different backgrounds from Charlotte's Irish Brontë peasant stock but they became close friends. Miss Wooler too remained a life-long friend of Charlotte.

After a year at Roe Head, when Charlotte was at Haworth for the Christmas holiday, she wrote a poem in which she described the destruction of Great Glass Town by the four Genii, and it seems probable that the children then decided to bring the Angria sagas to an end. Branwell and Charlotte soon

The Rydings, Birtstall, Ellen Nussey's home, on which Mr. Rochester's house Thornfield is at least partly based.

'It was three stories high, of proportions not vast, though considerable: a gentleman's manor-house, not a nobleman's seat: battlements round the top gave it a picturesque look. Its grey front stood out well from the background of a rookery, whose cawing tenants were now on the wing: they flew over the lawn and grounds to alight in a great meadow, from which these were separated by a sunk fence and where an array of mighty old thorn trees, strong, knotty, and broad as oaks, at once explained the etymology of the mansion's designation. Farther off were hills: not so lofty as those round Lowood, nor so craggy, not so like barriers of separation from the living world; but yet quiet and lonely hills enough, and seeming to embrace Thornfield with a seclusion I had not expected to find existent so near the stirring locality of Millcote.'

reversed this decision, Branwell writing many volumes, some in letter form, which when Charlotte returned, she developed into a more mature form of fantasy. However, it was while Charlotte was at Roe Head that Emily and Anne ended their contributions to the Great Glass Town stories and concentrated instead on their Gondal creations. This was a more romantic and poetic world, strongly influenced by their reading of Byron, and in sharp contrast to the military campaigns and political intrigue which their elder siblings brought to their stories of Angria.

Charlotte remained at Roe Head for only 18 months, leaving in July 1832, by which time she had completed the school's course of lessons, achieved some confidence and independence and gained the basic requirements to fit her to become a governess. However, she did not look for immediate employment. Instead, she now assumed this role at home, in Haworth, instructing her younger sisters.

In response to a letter from Ellen asking how she spent her time back at the Parsonage, she wrote:

'... an account of one day is an account of all. In the morning from 9 o'clock to half past 12, I instruct my sisters and draw, then we walk till dinner, after dinner I sew till tea time, and after tea I either read, write, do a little fancy work or draw, as I please. Thus in one delightful, though somewhat monotonous course, my life is passed.'

She did not tell Ellen what she wrote. Angria remained a secret (indeed she did not reveal her later pseudonymous authorship until after Ellen had made her criticisms of *Jane Eyre* known.)

Patrick Brontë encouraged his children's drawing, for a time paying a painter from Keighley to come and give them lessons. Many of their drawings are copies of engraved book illustra

tions, topographical studies in which each etched line is matched by a tiny pencil stroke, a concentration on minute detail that matches their volumes of minuscule writing. They developed some skill, painting each other, their pets and other animals and the familar places around them. Patrick Brontë hoped that his son's talent would enable him to make painting his profession.

There were music lessons too. Charlotte's poor sight was a slight drawback but the other girls became

pianists of some accomplishment and Branwell learned to play the flute and organ.

Ellen issued an invitation for Charlotte to visit her family, which was taken up in September 1832. Branwell drove his sister in a two-wheeled gig from Haworth for this first visit to Rydings, the Nussey home near Birstall. Ellen found him 'taking views in every direction of the old turret-roofed house, the fine chestnut trees on the lawns and a large rookery.' He thought that if his sister could not be happy in this 'paradise' she never would be anywhere.

During her stay Charlotte 'liked to pace the plantations or seek seclusion in the fruit garden'. Later, she almost certainly found a part model for Thornfield Hall in *Jane Eyre* in the Nussey house and a terrible thunderstorm which occurred during her stay may have provided the idea for the scene following Mr. Rochester's proposal of marriage, with its storm and stricken chestnut tree.

There were to be other visits to stay

The Red House, at Gomersal, home of the Taylor family, on which Charlotte Brontë based Briarmains, the home of Mr. Yorke in *Shirley*.

'... a hoar frost was insidiously stealing over growing grass and unfolding bud. It whitened the pavement in front of Briarmains (Mr. Yorke's residence), and made silent havoc among the tender plants of his garden, and on the mossy level of his lawn. As to that great tree, strong-trunked and broad-armed, which guarded the gable nearest the road, it seemed to defy a spring-night frost to harm its still bare boughs; and so did the leafless grove of walnut-trees rising tall behind the house.
In the dusk of the moonless if starry night, lights from windows shone vividly; this was no dark or lonely scene, nor even a silent one.
Briarmains stood near the highway, it was rather an old place, and had been built ere that highway was cut, and when a lane winding up through fields was the only path conducting to it. Briarfield lay scarce a mile off; its hum was heard, its glare distinctly seen.'
Shirley Chapter 9

The drawing-room of the Red House, Gomersal.

with Ellen, both at Rydings and at Brookroyd to which the Nusseys later moved. She stayed with the Taylors too, at the Red House, Gomersal (which was to be used as Briarmains in *Shirley*).

In July 1833, Ellen made her first visit to Haworth. Her reminiscences provide a picture of the house and its occupants at this time: the Reverend Brontë, venerable in appearance, courteous in manner and wearing a high white cravat, to which he gave a sem-

blance of freshness by winding new layers of white sewing silk over the old ones; Aunt Branwell, a small old lady, wearing huge caps, a 'false front' of light auburn curls peeping out beneath, her feet in wooden patterns to keep them off the cold stone floors, taking snuff from a gold box and nostalgic for the kinder climate of Penzance; and Tabby, faithful and dependable. Branwell she does not describe – he was then just 16, but this is how she remembered his younger sisters, Emily, 15 at the end of

The non-conformist chapel near the Red House, Gomersal.

'Briar Chapel, a large, new, raw, Wesleyan place of worship, rose but a few hundred yards distant [from Briarmains]; and, as there was even now a prayer-meeting being held within its walls, the illumination of its windows cast a bright reflection on the road ...'

Shirley Chapter 9

the month, who had already outgrown her brother, and 13-year-old Anne, both of whom she then met for the first time:

'Emily Brontë had by this time acquired a lithesome, graceful figure. She was the tallest person in the house, except for her father. Her hair, which was naturally as beautiful as Charlotte's, was in the same unbecoming tight curl and frizz, and there was the same want of complexion. She had very beautiful eyes – kind, kindling, liquid eyes; but she did not often look at you; she was too reserved ... their colour might be said to be dark grey, at other times dark blue, they varied so. She talked very little. She and Anne were like twins – inseparable companions, and in the very closest sympathy, which never had

any interruptions.

'Anne – dear, gentle Anne – was quite different in appearance from the others. She was her aunt's favourite. Her hair was a very pretty, light brown, and fell on her neck in graceful curls. She had lovely violet-blue eyes, fine pencilled eyebrows, and a clear, almost transparent complexion. She still pursued her studies, and especially her sewing, under the surveillance of her aunt. Emily had begun to have the disposal of her own time.'

In September, Branwell and Charlotte travelled by gig to Bolton Abbey, Wharfedale, to meet Ellen and her brothers and to dine at the Devonshire Arms. But he was awkward in such company, though socially superior to his plebian companions at the Black Bull. Branwell was developing a growing enthusiasm for music but in 1834, Reverend Brontë, who had hopes for Branwell's artistic talents, took all the children to an art exhibition in Leeds and later arranged for one of the exhibitors, William Robinson, to give them lessons, concentrating on Branwell. It was planned that Branwell would then continue his training at the Royal Academy Schools in London.

How were his fees and those for formal teaching for the younger girls to be met? Charlotte was to go away as a governess when another plan offered itself. She would teach at Roe Head with Miss Wooler and Emily would have a place at the school as part of her remuneration. Charlotte returned to Roe Head with Emily in July 1835. Emily was now 17 but this was the first time she had lived away from the family since the days at Cowan Bridge. Charlotte worried that she seemed

The Black Bull, on Haworth's main street and beside the steps leading to the church. Branwell Brontë joined the Haworth Temperance Society at the end of 1834 and became its secretary (his father was president) – but that did not stop him drinking. The Bull was one place where he could escape from his melancholy sense of failure and among its patrons he gained a reputation for fine conversation and social ease.

unwell and realized that the cause was homesickness and the constraints of boarding-school life:

'Liberty was the breath of Emily's nostrils: without it she perished. The change from her own home to a school, and from her own very noiseless, very secluded, but unrestricted and inartificial mode of life, to one of disciplined routine (though under the kindest auspices) was what she failed in enduring. Her nature proved here too strong for her fortitude. Every morning when she woke, the vision of home and the moors rushed on her, and darkened and saddened the day that lay before her. Nobody knew what ailed her but me – I knew only too well. In this struggle her health was quickly broken; her white-faced, attenuated form, and failing strength threatened rapid decline. I felt in my heart she would die, if she did not go home, and with this conviction obtained her recall.'

In October, only three months after arriving at the school, Emily returned to Haworth. The following January, Anne went to Roe Head in her place.

William Robinson, meanwhile, had made arrangements for Branwell to seek admission to the Royal Academy Schools, and provided him with letters of introduction. Aunt Branwell provided him with money. While Emily was at Roe Head, or perhaps early in 1836, he set off on the two-day coach journey to London. He certainly got there, but there is no evidence that he ever presented himself at the Royal Academy or used any of his letters of introduction. He returned to Haworth with a tale that he had been set upon by thieves and his money stolen before he even reached London. A fellow Yorkshireman later claimed to have met him in the Castle Tavern in High Holborn, kept by a famous boxer called Tom Spring – a hero of the 18-year-old member of Haworth Boxing Club.

An Angria story, written by Branwell in 1836, may be a clue to what happened: a visitor to London is so overcome by the scale of the dome of St. Paul's Cathedral that he hardly dares enter the building. His senses assaulted by the city, he lapses into meaningless wandering and the solace of 'squibs of rum'. Was it the Castle Tavern or the Royal Academy that Branwell found overwhelming? Had his money been stolen, lost, gambled or drunk away? Was his explanation accepted by his father and Aunt Branwell? Certainly any thought of the Academy was dropped. Branwell wrote

A tree on Haworth Moor, its shape conforming to the prevailing winds. Even when they were away from Haworth the Brontës felt drawn to their native moors. Charlotte writes in a letter when away from home:

'... that wind, pouring in impetuous current through the air, sounding wildly, unremittingly from hour to hour, deepening its tone as the night advances, coming not in gusts, but with a rapid gathering stormy swell – that wind I know is heard at this moment far away in the moors of Haworth. Branwell and Emily hear it, and as it sweeps over our house, down the churchyard, and round the old church, they think perhaps of me and Anne.'

poems and made some attempts to get published in *Blackwood's Magazine*, but his letters to them met with no response, though they were kept as curiosities as originating from a possible lunatic.

There is a tradition, though no firm evidence, that Branwell was for a short time an usher at a school near Halifax but left, or was told to leave, after only one term. Then in May 1838 he set up a studio in Bradford, walking home at weekends across the moors, or sometimes taking a coach to Keighley. He hoped to make a living painting portraits, but it was not the best time to do so; the novelty of photography had arrived as a way of making 'likenesses'.

Anne Brontë settled in at Roe Head far better than Emily had and proved a diligent pupil, though the winter of 1836-7 found her depressed and unwell and the teacher-pupil divide made it difficult for Charlotte to help her. Charlotte herself became increasingly dissatisfied with her duties which gave her little time to escape into her literary fantasy world. During the summer she had been rewriting some of Branwell's work in verse form and thought of a career in poetry. She wrote to Robert Southey, then Poet Laureate, asking his advice. His stern answer warned her against 'the day-dreams in which you habitually indulge' and patronizingly declared that:

'*Literature cannot be the business of a woman's life, and it ought not to be. The more she is engaged in her proper duties, the less leisure she will have for it, even as an accomplishment and recreation.*'

Southey, of course, knew only what she told him of her circumstances. Her frustration can be seen in the subtext of her reply:

'*You do not forbid me to write; you do not say that what I write is utterly destitute of merit. You only warn me against the folly of neglecting real duties for the sake of imaginative pleasures; of writing for the love of fame; for the selfish excitement of emulation. You kindly allow me to write poetry for its own sake, provided I have undone nothing which I ought to do, in order to pursue that single, absorbing, exquisite gratification. I am afraid, sir, you think me very foolish. I know the first letter I wrote you was all senseless trash from beginning to end; but I am not altogether the idle, dreaming being it would seem to denote ... I don't always succeed (in discharging her feminine duty), for sometimes when I'm teaching or sewing I would rather be reading or writing; but I try to deny myself.*'

The death of Miss Wooler's father and various domestic rearrangements led, in the summer of 1837, to the school being relocated at Heald's House, Dewsbury Moor. Charlotte disliked the place, and, to make matters worse, Miss Wooler, being often away on family business, her responsibilities increased and became even more onerous.

Towards the end of the year Anne was taken ill at school and Charlotte, seeing her in pain and breathing with difficulty was understandably agitated, especially after what had happened to her elder sisters. Miss Wooler viewed Anne's situation less gravely. As Charlotte wrote to Ellen Nussey:

'*Miss Wooler thought me a fool, and by way of proving her opinion treated me with marked coldness. We came to a little éclairissement one evening. I told her one or two rather plain truths, which set her a-crying, and the next day unknown to me, she wrote to Papa telling him that I had reproached her bitterly – taken her severely to task, etc. etc. Papa sent for us the day after he received her letter.*'

Anne was brought home in December and, though Charlotte healed the rift with Margaret Wooler, she determined that she would give up the post as soon as possible. Her own health and spirits were at low ebb and on medical advice, she resigned and left the school in May 1838.

Emily had thrived back home in Haworth, writing poems, teaching herself French and German and, when Tabitha Aykroyd broke her leg just before Christmas 1836, taking charge of the kitchen. But in the autumn of 1837, she accepted a post teaching at a girls' school at Law Hill, at Southowram, on one of the hills surrounding Halifax.

She found teaching drudgery. 'Hard labour from six in the morning until near eleven at night, with only one half-hour of exercise in between. This is slavery,' commented Charlotte, 'I fear she will never stand it.' But she did, though for how long is uncertain. For six months, definitely, perhaps for a year and a half, the evidence is unclear, but time enough to get to know some of the surrounding countryside, perhaps on horseback, riding being part of the school curriculum. She makes use of local features in *Wuthering Heights*.

Anne, too, found the courage to make her own way, securing a position as a governess to the children of Mrs. Ingham, of Blake Hall, Mirfield in April 1839. She found that Mrs. Ingham spoiled the children and the problems of the post are echoed in the first part of *Agnes Grey* (though if she followed the methods Agnes uses we might not have had much sympathy with her). She stayed nine months before the post was terminated prior to the Christmas holidays.

Charlotte stayed an even shorter time when she went as governess to the Sidgwick family at Stonegappe, near Skipton, in May. The house was in a beautiful setting but the children were 'riotous, perverse, unmanageable cubs'. There were innumerable visitors and she was expected to take on a heavy load of 'plain sewing' as part of her duties. She was allowed no time to herself and was able to tolerate it only until July.

Before taking up the post Charlotte had had an offer of marriage, from Ellen Nussey's brother Henry. She turned him down, wisely perhaps, since he had made a similar proposal to two other ladies, one of them only two days earlier! Now came another proposal, received by post from an Irish curate who met her one day when on a visit to her father. His jokes had made her laugh, as possibly did his ardent letter, but she promptly refused him too.

The arrival of the flirtatious William Weightman as Mr. Brontë's curate, in August 1839, added a little spice to parsonage life; Anne's poetry suggests that she fell in love with him, though how deeply is uncertain.

For part of 1839 and after Charlotte's return from Dewsbury Moor until Anne took up another governess post at Thorpe Green not far from York, in August 1840, all three sisters were at home together at Haworth. Branwell too, was back at Haworth from May of 1839. He had made some friends in Bradford, including the sculptor J.B. Leyland, and was popular in public houses where he

Law Hill, which was the school at Southowram, east of Halifax, where Emily took a teaching job.

A watercolour of Keeper, the parsonage house-dog, painted by Emily Brontë who was particularly fond of him. She dated it 24 April 1838 and labels it 'from life', so she must have been back at Haworth at this time.

gained a reputation for his sparkling conversation. He had found some clients for portraits, but there had not been nearly enough.

At home, Branwell was further coached in the classics by his father, but such education, however appropriate for a gentleman, did not seem to be preparing him for earning a living. Nevertheless, it did have its uses, for he too found a post as tutor to the sons of a Mr. Postlethwaite of Broughton-on-Furness. He joined their household in the New Year of 1840 and found life not too exacting; he even had time to work on his translation of the *Odes of Horace* – completing all but one. Sending copies of two translations and one of his own poems to Hartley Coleridge (son of the poet Samuel Taylor Coleridge), whom he had met in Bradford, he received an invitation to visit his home by Rydal Water. Coleridge encouraged his writing (unlike his father's friend Wordsworth to whom Branwell had also written earlier), and this is perhaps what led him to neglect his duties as a tutor. He came home late, sometimes rather drunk, and when it was discovered that he spent much of his lesson time drawing and telling stories to fit the pictures, he was dismissed. He managed to present himself to his sisters as hard-done-by, which from their experience as governesses they were inclined to believe.

In September 1840, he made another fresh start, securing a post as assistant clerk at the railway station at Sowerby Bridge in the Calder Valley, on a newly opened stretch of the Leeds-Manchester Railway. The first passenger railway, hauled by steam-locomotives, had opened only 15 years before and this was a time when railways were rapidly being built all over Britain.

His friend Leyland lived in Halifax,

only two miles away, and he made other friends, enjoying walks with them in the valley and its surrounding hills in his off-duty hours. A few months later, when the line was extended further, he was moved up-line a mile to Luddenden Foot where he was made clerk-in-charge. Ellen Nussey wrote to Charlotte with her congratulations on the news, but Charlotte replied with an ominous italic: 'it *looks* like promotion...' But if she was uncertain there was no doubt that his salary had been increased

Stonegappe, Lothersdale, near Skipton, where Charlotte spent a short and stressful time as governess.

from £75 to £130 per annum.

The station house had not yet been built, so Branwell took lodgings in the village. His duties were not onerous and he had time for writing. Leyland's brother Francis (later Branwell's biographer) helped him get some poems published in *The Halifax Guardian*. A local poet, William Heaton, described him at this time as:

'blithe and gay, but at times appeared downcast and sad; yet, if the subject were some topic that he was acquainted with, or some author he loved, he would rise from his seat, and, in beautiful language, describe the author's character, with a zeal and fluency I have never heard equalled. His talents were of a very exalted kind. I have heard him quote pieces from the bard of Avon, from Shelley, Wordsworth, and Byron, as well as from Butler's 'Hudibras', in such a manner as often made me wish I had been a scholar, as he was.'

Neither challenged nor engrossed by his work, Branwell became careless.

Sowerby Bridge, in the Calder Valley, where Branwell Brontë had his first railway job.

Much of his time was passed at the Lord Nelson Inn, where the attractions were a lending library, cheap ale and good company. When the railway managers made an audit of his books they found that he was £11.1s.7d short. He was not accused of dishonesty but the

drawings, doodlings and pieces of verse that appeared among the railway records, and reported absences from the station, showed an unacceptable carelessness and in March 1842 he was dismissed.

In contrast to Heaton's picture of

Sowerby Bridge, in the Calder Valley, where Branwell Brontë had his first railway job.

him, Branwell later wrote of this time, with his usual romantic dramatization: '*I would rather give my hand than undergo again the grovelling carelessness, the malignant yet cold debauchery, the determination to find how far mind could carry body without being chucked into hell,*' *which too often marked my conduct, when there, lost as I was to all I really liked ...*'

Meanwhile, back at Haworth, the curate, William Weightman, a good scholar (which commended him to Mr. Brontë), and a lively companion to the girls, who dubbed him Miss Celia

Luddenden Dean. Branwell was put in charge of the station at Luddenden Foot.

Amelia and called him by that odd epithet, also befriended Branwell. He might have proved a major influence in helping this clever but muddled young man to make something out of his life but in the autumn of 1842 he died of cholera, aged only 26. The parish erected a monument inside the church to extol his virtues.

Haworth Churchyard from the tower of St. Michael's church. After Rev. Brontë's curate William Weightman died, Anne Brontë wrote these lines, probably in memory of him:
Yes, thou art gone, and never more
Thy sunny smile shall gladden me
But I may pass the old church door
And pace the floor that covers thee
May stand upon the cold, damp stone
And think that, frozen, lies below
The lightest heart that I have ever known,
The kindest I shall ever know.

A SCHOOL OF THEIR OWN?

I am miserable when I allow myself to dwell on the necessity of spending my life as a governess. The chief requisite for that station seems to me to be the power of taking things easily as they come, and of making oneself comfortable and at home wherever we may chance to be – qualities in which all our family are singularly deficient.'

Thus wrote Charlotte Brontë when she was at Stonegappe with the Sidgwicks. But in March 1841 she took up yet another post as governess, this time to a family called White at Upperworth House, Rawdon, northeast of Bradford. Although she found herself expected to do far too much sewing and snobbishly thought Mrs. White low class, she found this post much more congenial, not least because her employers were often away. During three weeks of spring cleaning, when the nursemaid took over the duties of cook and maid, she had to be nurse as well as governess but, she told Ellen Nussey:

'I have managed to get a good deal more control over the children this makes my life a good deal easier; also by dint of nursing the fat baby, it has got to know me and be fond of me. I suspect myself of growing rather fond of it.'

Charlotte demanded a holiday in July and, in those three weeks with Emily (Anne was still at Thorpe Green), hatched the idea of starting a school of their own. Aunt Branwell promised financial help and Margaret Wooler suggested that they might take over the school at Heald's House when

her sister could be persuaded to retire. Charlotte accepted this offer, but wrote in September with another idea, prompted in part by the Whites who had suggested that Emily and herself go abroad to improve their qualifications before entering the competitive market for pupils. Various places were discussed but a letter from Mary Taylor, extolling the cathedrals and paintings she was seeing with her brother while travelling in Belgium and Holland and the fact that her sister Martha was at school near Brussels, confirmed their choice of that city, though they would have to find a cheaper school than the fashionable one which Martha attended.

Charlotte and Emily arranged to become boarders at a school run by Mme. Heger-Parent. Charlotte left the Whites on Christmas Eve and in February 1842, their father escorted Charlotte and Emily to London. There they stayed in Paternoster Row at the Chapter Coffee House, where Mr. Brontë had stayed many years before and had instructed Branwell to stay on his London visit.

After three days of sight-seeing with Mary and Joseph Taylor, they took the London-Ostend steam-packet and after spending a night at the home of the chaplain at the British Embassy, they were delivered by their father to *La Maison d'Éducation pour les Jeunes Demoiselles* at 32, rue d'Isabelle. Their experiences there were to provide material for *Villette* and *The Professor*.

Charlotte wrote to Ellen Nussey

that they had 'got into a very good school – and are considerably comfortable.' With the snobbish sense of superiority that had made her criticize Mrs. White, she looked down on the French mistresses, the Belgian girls and their Catholicism, and resented the careful surveillance of Mme. Heger-Parent but, at least at first, seemed very happy in Brussels. Emily was less outgoing when they were entertained by other English residents and generally unpopular, except with some of the younger pupils who liked her better than Charlotte.

M. Heger, who taught literature at the nearby boys' school, the *Athénée Royale*, gave lessons in between his work there and found time for special classes for Charlotte and Emily, to the envy of the other pupils. Their studies went well and they stayed in Brussels for the summer holiday. The school proposed that they should stay on for another six months and that, instead of paying for their board and tuition, they would become part-time teachers: Emily would give music classes and Charlotte teach English. This arrangement began well but, in November, there came news from Haworth of Aunt Branwell's death and they felt bound to return home at once.

M. Heger wrote appreciatively that he hoped they would both be able to complete their course and promised that he would be able to offer a full teaching post to one of them at the end of the year. Emily preferred to stay at Haworth to keep house for her father, but in January 1843, Charlotte returned to Brussels as a teacher, her duties including English lessons for M. Heger and his brother-in-law. Now she began to find the Hegers the only people for whom she could 'experience regard and esteem', life was boring and monotonous and she felt isolated and lonely, especially as a lone Protestant among

Catholics. Martha Taylor had died of cholera in Brussels the previous autumn and Mary had left for Germany. There were some other English friends but they were away during the summer and the loneliness became worse. Charlotte's feelings were also complicated by a strong romantic and, perhaps, sexual attraction to M. Heger which, as it became clear to Mme. Heger, caused that lady to become colder towards her and to end the gentlemen's English lessons. Charlotte left Brussels before the year was out, declaring: 'However long I live, I shall not forget what the parting with M. Heger cost me ... so true, kind and disinterested a friend.' She continued to write effusive letters to him long after he had stopped replying.

With Emily at home, Branwell was able to take up a post offered by Anne's employers, the Robinsons, as tutor to their son, while Anne continued to teach their three girls. His personality and scholarship seem to have charmed Mrs. Robinson and Branwell, perhaps misjudging the nature of her attentions to him, fell in love with her. He later claimed that this married lady, 12 years his senior, loved him from first meeting. Was this a delusion or was there a real affair? Whatever the situation all seems to have gone well there at first and he held the post longer than any other.

When Charlotte returned to Haworth, her father's sight began to deteriorate rapidly, causing him to rely more and more upon his curates. Haworth seemed dull after Brussels, but she felt it would be wrong to leave home now and began to develop plans to run a school for five or six pupils at the Parsonage, a number which they could expand by building onto the house should the plan be successful. A prospectus was printed in the summer and distributed. Charlotte wrote letters

Church Lane, Haworth. The
Parsonage is on the left, the Sunday
School right. Both Charlotte and
Branwell taught at the School; he had
no patience with slow pupils.

to previous employers and parents of potential pupils. There was no response, the bleak location of Haworth itself probably being the main deterrent, and by the summer Emily was noting that she and her sisters no longer had 'any great longing for it. We have cash enough for our present wants, with a prospect of accumulation ...' They had indeed, their inheritance from their aunt. But by the end of the autumn the plans for a school were abandoned.

In March 1845, Charlotte made a visit to Hunsworth to stay with Mary Taylor, who was about to emigrate to New Zealand. In June, Anne having come home for a holiday decided not to go back to the Robinsons; she felt she should take a further break at Hathersage to help Ellen Nussey prepare the vicarage for her brother Henry, who had found a bride at last – and a rich one, and was away on honeymoon. At the end of June, it was the turn of Emily and Anne to make a brief trip to York, leaving Tabitha in charge.

On her return to Haworth, Charlotte found Branwell at home, ill – perhaps a euphemism for drunk. He had come home because the Robinsons had gone on holiday to Scarborough. Something had been confessed or discovered there which had caused Mr. Robinson to send him a stern note of dismissal, 'charging him on pain of exposure to break off instantly and forever all communication with every member of his family'.

What could have been exposed? Branwell's version was that he had been having a long and passionate love affair with Lydia Robinson, two years of 'troubled pleasure soon chastised by fear'. Was this an exaggeration on Branwell's part, even an invention to cover some other misdemeanour? The letter of dismissal was sent the day after Robinson's son, who had stayed on at home with Branwell, arrived in Scarborough: could the dismissal have been linked to conduct with the boy?

Was Anne aware of a liaison and had it influenced her decision not to return to Thorpe Park, or did she only hear Branwell's version? Both Branwell and Anne echo the affair in their fiction, he depicting himself as the seducer in *And the Weary are at Rest*, while she, in *The Tenant of Wildfell Hall*, puts the blame squarely on the lady, seeming to believe her brother to have been the victim.

Branwell claimed that he continued to receive money sent by Mrs. Robinson. He may also have borrowed on the expectation of wealth were they to have married on her widowhood. He claimed that, following her husband's death in 1846, she sent a message saying they must never meet again, for by her husband's will she would lose her fortune if they married, warning him never to see her again, or a condition in her husband's will would cut her off with nothing. She certainly didn't seem to be contemplating marriage with Branwell.

Whatever the balance of fact and self-delusion, Branwell came to believe his own version, and, though still making some attempt to write, resorted increasingly to drink and opium to cushion the disappointments of his life. Romantics see his degeneration as the cracking of a broken heart. His sisters were forced to endure all this. A few weeks later, Charlotte reported that he had demanded money from his father with threats of suicide.

One evening, probably drunk or drugged, Branwell passed out in his room and dropped a journal he had been reading on to a candle, which in turn set fire to his bed curtains. Emily discovered him and flung a bucket of water over the flames; but thereafter he spent his nights in his father's bedroom. His health suffered but, two years later, there was little warning when he died suddenly of consumption, probably unaware that, by then, his sisters had all achieved successful publication. Mrs. Gaskell gave credence to a local rumour that he stood up to die with letters from Mrs. Robinson spilling from his pockets. Soon afterwards, Lydia Robinson married the newly-widowed Sir Edward Scott.

Difficult though life must have been, coping with Branwell's drunkeness and rages and caring for their near-blind father, the sisters' lives were now briefly to take a more positive direction.

PUBLICATION

On Haworth Moor.
In *Wuthering Heights,* Mr. Lockwood soon discovers the sudden changes which can be brought about by winter on the moors:
'*... the whole hill-back was one billowy, white ocean; the swells and falls not indicating corresponding rises and depressions in the ground: many pits, at least, were filled to a level; and entire ranges of mounds, the refuse of the quarries, blotted from the chart which*

In February 1844, not long after Charlotte's return from Brussels, Emily began to make fresh copies of her poems into two notebooks, one of them reserved for her Gondal poems. The sisters did not share their private writing with each other but Charlotte came across one of these notebooks in the autumn of the following year and was impressed by the quality of Emily's work. She considered these poems deserving of publication. Emily was furious when she learned that her privacy had been breached, but was eventually won over. Anne produced some of her verse and allowed Charlotte to select poems from it, who in turn added poems of her own and a joint publication was prepared. Emily insisted on using pen names and they decided to

take seemingly masculine ones, partly because it was thought that male poets met with less prejudice and partly because they did not consider their work to be obviously 'feminine'. They called themselves Currer, Ellis and Acton Bell.

Aylott & Jones, a London publisher specializing in religious poetry, agreed to bring the book out at the authors' expense: ten pounds each at first, plus a further single sum of five pounds. Charlotte was involved in considerable correspondence concerning the format, paper, typography and there was discussion as to whom should be sent copies for review. At length, towards the end of May 1846, the blue-bound volume appeared.

This volume of poetry had favourable reviews in *The Atheneum* and *The Dublin University Magazine* but after two months, only two copies had been sold. The book was a financial failure but the sisters were not discouraged; they had also been engaged on other work, novels which had, perhaps, been begun earlier. Anne had completed *Agnes Grey* and Charlotte *The Professor*, both drawing very directly on their own experiences, while Emily's *Wuthering Heights* used the background of the moors and plot details culled from true stories she had heard. Manuscripts of all these novels were already on their way to a publisher.

my yesterday's walk had pictured in my mind. I had remarked on one side of the road, at intervals of six or seven yards, a line of upright stones, continued through the whole length of the barren: these were erected and daubed with lime on purpose to serve as guides in the dark, and also when a fall, like the present, confounded the deep swamps on either hand with the firmer path: but, excepting a dirty dot pointing up here and there, all traces of their existence had vanished ...'
Wuthering Heights Chapter 3

Patrick Brontë, now nearly 70, knew nothing of all this; his sight was affected by cataracts and for almost a year he had been unable to see, write or walk without a guide. Emily and Charlotte discovered a surgeon in Manchester who they thought might be able to operate to remove the cataract from one eye. After an examination, arrangements were made for the operation to take place in August 1846, and Charlotte and her father took lodgings in Manchester. At his request, she stayed with him and held his hand during the operation, which was performed without anaesthetic.

For a month he was obliged to rest in a darkened room in Manchester, but the operation was a success. Charlotte, awaiting her father's recovery, was suffering from nagging toothache and sought distraction from her pain and boredom by starting a new novel: the story of *Jane Eyre*.

A small publisher called T.C. Newby offered to publish *Wuthering Heights* and *Agnes Grey* in a single volume, provided the authors would advance £50, but he rejected *The Professor* as too acerbic. It was turned down by four more publishing houses before it arrived at Smith, Elder & Company in a wrapper, the crossed-out addresses indicating that it had been the rounds. However, it was given to their reader who recognized its 'great literary power' and, though rejecting it 'for business reasons', wrote an appreciative letter and indicated that a three-volume work by the author would receive their careful attention. Charlotte had by then almost completed *Jane Eyre* and it was sent to Smith, Elder in July 1847. Years later publisher George Smith recollected receiving Charlotte's manuscript. *'After breakfast on Sunday morning I took the MS of Jane Eyre to my little study and began to read it. The story quickly took me*

captive. *Before twelve o'clock my horse came to the door (he had planned to go riding with a friend) but I could not put the book down. I scribbled [a note of apology] and went on reading the MS. Presently the servant came to tell me that luncheon was ready. I asked him to bring me a sandwich and a glass of wine and still I went on with Jane Eyre. Dinner came; for me the meal was a very hasty one, and before I went to bed I had finished reading the manuscript.*

'The next day we wrote to Currer Bell accepting the book for publication.'

Jane Eyre was published in October. It sold well and was reviewed enthusiastically; within months it was being reprinted. Anne and Emily's books followed from Newby in December but did not have the same success. Charlotte offered to rewrite The Professor but her publisher, though wanting another book from her, still refused it, and it was not published until after her death. A serial was proposed, but Charlotte felt happier with a three-volume novel.

In October, Charlotte gave her father a copy of her book which he read and excitedly declared 'much better than likely'. Thus he discovered his daughters' literary achievements in which he later took great pride.

Meanwhile, her sisters' publisher encouraged the confusion between the various Bells. Anne had sent him her second novel The Tenant of Wildfell Hall, which he brought out in June 1848 offering it to an American publisher as the work of Currer Bell and claiming that all the Bells were one and the same person.

George Smith wrote to 'Currer Bell' to establish the truth. Charlotte decided they should go immediately to London and clear the matter up. Emily refused to go but she and Anne presented themselves at the publisher's office and, refusing to give his clerk their names, asked to see him on a private matter.

The Worth Valley from Ponden Kirk.
'... a golden afternoon of August: every breath from the hills so full of life, that it seemed whoever respired it, though dying, might revive. Catherine's face was just like the landscape – shadows and sunshine flitting over it in rapid succession; but the shadows rested longer, and the sunshine was more transient ...'
Wuthering Heights Chapter 27

BELOW
Haworth Moor with Top Withens on the horizon.

BELOW RIGHT
The site of Top Withens farmhouse, fallen into ruin in the present century but occupied in the Brontës' time, is widely thought to have suggested the location of Wuthering Heights, though not the house itself.

On being shown into his office they presented the envelope, addressed in his own hand to 'Currer Bell Esq.' Smith later described how, when confronted by 'two rather quaintly dressed little ladies' he 'noticed that the letter had been opened, and said with some sharpness, "Where did you get this?" "From the Post Office," was the reply, "it was addressed to me. We have both come that you might have occular proof that there are at least two of us." '

Charlotte unintentionally let slip that there were three sisters and, since she had not got Emily's permission to disclose her identity, was forced to qualify the admission and appeal to Smith to keep Ellis Bell's identity a secret.

The sisters, exhausted after a sleepless journey south – they had travelled by railway on the night express – retired to their lodgings. But Smith, eager to entertain his best-selling authoress sappropriately, arrived with his bejewelled and evening-gowned sisters to whisk them off on a surprise visit to the opera.

Before they returned to Haworth, Charlotte and Anne had been to Sunday service to hear a fashionable preacher, visited W.S. Williams and his family, inspected the exhibition at the Royal Academy and seen the collection at the National Gallery. They made firm friends of Charlotte's publishers, who began to send regular parcels of new books and literary reviews to Haworth.

Smith, Elder set about buying up the remaining copies of the 'Bell brothers' ' poems and made plans to reissue them. They had *three* talented new writers on their list of authors – success was beginning to shine on the Brontës – but dark clouds were closing in to destroy their happiness.

ABOVE
Ponden Kirk, the outcrop of rock
which becomes the Penistone Crags
of *Wuthering Heights*.
'The abrupt descent of Penistone Crags
particularly attracted her notice,
especially when the setting sun shone on
it, and the topmost heights; and the
whole extent of the landscape besides
lay in shadow.
'I explained that they were masses of
stone, with hardly enough earth in
their clefts to nourish a stunted tree.
"And why are they so bright so long
after it is evening here?" she pursued.
"Because they are a great deal higher
up than we are," replied I; "you could
not climb them, they are too high and
steep. In winter the frost is always
there before it comes to us; and deep
into summer, I have found snow under
that black hollow on the
north-east side." '
Wuthering Heights Chapter 18

LEFT
Ponden Hall, in the Worth valley
below Top Withens, and on the road
from Haworth to Wycoller, stands near
the shores of Ponden Reservoir. It is
generally identified as the location in
which Thrushcross Grange was
imagined, but this is nothing like the
building described in
Wuthering Heights.
'Wuthering Heights is the name of Mr.
Heathcliff's dwelling. "Wuthering"
being a significant provincial adjec-
tive, descriptive of the atmospheric
tumult to which its station is exposed in
stormy weather. Pure, bracing
ventilations they must have up there at
all times, indeed: one may guess by the
power of the north wind blowing over
the edge, by the excessive slant of a few
stunted firs at the end of the house; and
by a range of gaunt thorns all
stretching their limbs one way, as if
craving alms of the sun.'
Wuthering Heights Chapter 1

LEFT
Shibden Hall, near Halifax, visible on
the opposite escarpment from Law Hill
School, where Emily taught, is one
candidate as a model for Thrushcross
Grange. The sculptural details of the
entrance a 'wilderness of crumbling
griffons and shameless little boys' was
probably suggested by another
mansion above it on the top of the
escarpment: High Sutherland Hall,
now demolished.

On 24 September came Branwell's sudden death – a release from the stress and horror that his unhappy behaviour had brought about, but devastating to his father and sisters. At the funeral, Emily caught a cold. She had tuberculosis, like her brother, but went on with her domestic chores, at first refusing even to see a doctor. She died on 19 December, never to know how highly *Wuthering Heights* would later come to be regarded: depression at its failure and sorrow at Branwell's passing were quite likely to have been responsible for accelerating her own death.

Soon it became clear that Anne also had tuberculosis. She dutifully followed the medical instructions given by the specialist Dr. Teale, who had been called in from Leeds, but was obviously deteriorating. She had a wish to visit Scarborough, which she already knew from visits with the Robinsons. The doctor had at first forbidden travel but now reluctantly approved the idea and it was there that Charlotte and Ellen Nussey took her in the Spring of 1849. On the way they visited York so that she could see the Minster once again and then moved into rooms at Wood's

Ruined Wycoller Hall, eight miles west of Haworth. Its fireplace is cited as one of the reasons for identifying it as the model for Ferndean where Jane found Mr. Rochester after the disaster at Thornfield:

'*... you could see nothing of it, so thick and dark grew the timber of the gloomy wood about it. Iron gates between granite pillars showed me where to enter, and passing through them, I found myself at once in the twilight of close-ranked trees. There was a grass-grown track descending the forest aisle between hoar and knotty shafts and under branched arches. I followed it, expecting soon to reach the dwelling; but ... wound far and farther: no sign of habitation or grounds was visible.*

'*... at last my way opened, the trees thinned a little; presently I beheld a railing, then the house – scarce, by this dim light, distinguishable from the trees; so dank and green were its decaying walls. Entering a portal, fastened only by a latch, I stood amidst a space of enclosed ground, from which the wood swept away in a semi-circle. There were no flowers, no garden-beds; only a gravel-walk girdling a grass-plat, and this set in the heavy frame of the forest.*'
Jane Eyre Chapter 37

The towers of York Minster rise above the ancient city. The great cathedral so impressed Anne Brontë that she insisted Emily make a trip to see it and visited it again on her way to Scarborough during her final illness.

Lodgings on The Cliff at Scarborough. For three days she insisted on walking or driving on the sands, extracting every last moment of pleasure from her remaining hours and, after watching a glorious sunset, died quietly on 28 May. She was buried at Scarborough in St. Mary's churchyard, on the cliff below the castle.

Flamborough Head, between Scarborough and Bridlington.

Anne Brontë drew on her experience as a governess with the Robinsons and her observation of her brother's behaviour there and at home iwhen writing *The Tenant of Wildfell Hall*. Thorpe Green is northwest of York but Anne made visits to the coast, sespecially Scarborough, with her employers and Wildfell Hall is set only four miles from the sea. Helen Huntingdon and Gilbert Markham make a memorable trip to see a celebrated sea-view:

'The increasing height and boldness of the hills had for some time intercepted the prospect; but, on gaining the summit of a steep acclivity, and looking downward, an opening lay before us – and the blue sea burst upon our sight! – a deep violet blue – not deadly calm, but covered with glinting breakers – diminutive white specks twinkling on its bosom, and scarcely to be distinguished, by the keenest vision, from the little sea-mews that sported above, their white wings glittering in the sunshine: only one or two vessels were visible: and those were far away.'
The Tenant of Wildfell Hall Chapter 7

Scarborough harbour with its castle on the heights above.

The beach at Scarborough, one of Anne Brontë's last pleasures, which she enjoyed as much as did her heroine Agnes Grey:

'But the sea was my delight; and I would often gladly pierce the town to obtain the pleasure of a walk beside it ... It was delightful to me at all times and seasons, but especially in the wild commotion of a rough sea-breeze, and in the brilliant freshness of a summer morning.'
Agnes Grey Chaper 24

Anne Brontë's grave (foreground) is in the churchyard of St. Mary's, Scarborough, high on the cliffs below the castle.

Anne Brontë's grave.

'I was dressed and out when the church clock struck a quarter to six. There was a feeling of freshness and vigour in the very streets, and when I got free of the town, when my foot was on the sands and my face towards the broad, bright bay, no language can describe the effect of the deep, clear azure of the sky and ocean, the bright morning sunshine on the semi-circular barrier of craggy cliffs surmounted by green swelling hills, and on the smooth, wide sands, and the low rocks out at sea – looking, with their clothing of weeds and moss, like little grass-grown islands – and above all, on the brilliant, sparkling waves, and then, the unspeakable purity and freshness of the air! There was just enough heat to enhance the value of the breeze, and just enough wind to keep the whole sea in motion, to make the waves come bounding to the shore, foaming and sparkling, as if wild with glee. Nothing else was stirring – no living creature was visible besides myself. My footsteps were the first to press the firm, unbroken sands; – nothing before had trampled them since last night's flowing tide had obliterated the deepest marks of yesterday, and left it fair and even, except where the subsiding water had left behind it the traces of dimpled pools and little running streams.'
Agnes Grey Chapter 24

FAME AND MRS. NICHOLLS

Before the death of Branwell and the tragic months that followed, Charlotte had been working on *Shirley*, set in the area near Dewsbury which she knew from her time at Roe Head and her visits to the Nusseys and the Taylors. This was where her father had lived when he first came to Yorkshire. His memories of the Luddite risings against the growing mechanization of wool processing and cloth manufacture, four years before her birth, form the background to the story. To support what she had heard, she obtained newspaper reports from Leeds relating to the incidents at Hartshead. Shirley, herself, incorporates many of Emily's virtues, her dog Keeper finds a place and even her father's curate, Arthur Nicholls, appears as a character towards the end of the novel.

By the end of August *Shirley* was finished and one of Smith, Elder's staff came up to Haworth to collect it. It was published on 26 October 1849 to considerable acclaim, though not so highly praised as *Jane Eyre* had been. The identity of Currer Bell was now becoming more widely known. Some of her acquaintances recognized aspects of themselves or people they knew in her characters. The previous year, Charlotte had had a serious quarrel with Ellen Nussey when she intimated that she had heard that she had published a novel, writing:

'... *just say... that you are authorized by Miss Brontë to say that she repels and disowns every accusation of this kind. You*

may add, if you please, that if anyone has her confidence, you may believe you have, and that she had made no drivelling confessions to you on the subject.'

She still felt she could escape identification but her secret could be kept no

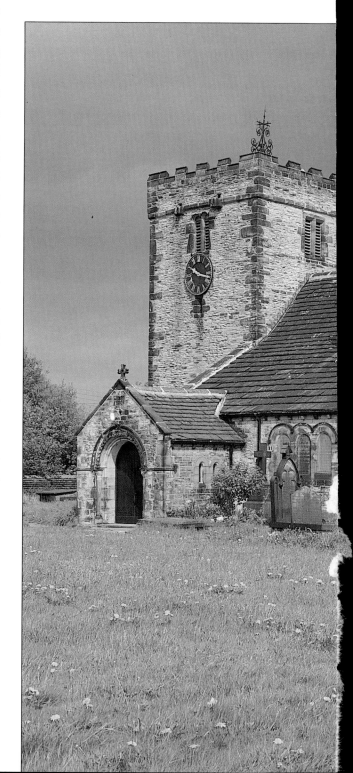

longer. The addressing of 'Mr Bell's' letters to the parsonage did not go unnoticed and soon local people were attempting to identify themselves in the characters of *Shirley*.

Over the next few years there were several trips to London to stay with George Smith at his mother's house in Gloucester Terrace, with introductions to critics and authors, visits to theatres and exhibitions, the Zoological Gardens, the Houses of Parliament and, for this was the time of the Great Exhibition, the Crystal Palace. On one occasion, at Mr. Smith's request, she sat for a portrait by George Richmond. Charlotte engaged in correspondence with several authors, including William Makepeace Thackery, whom she had long held in high esteem, and who now returned her admiration. She paid a visit to Edinburgh with Mr. Smith and his sisters and the retired Lancashire education reformer and philanthropist Sir James Kay-Shuttleworth called at Haworth to present an invitation for her to visit himself and his wife, which Mr. Brontë insisted she accept. Later

St. Peter's Church, Hartshead, four miles from Dewsbury and not far from Roe Head. It was Patrick Brontë's first independent curacy, before Charlotte was born. It becomes the Nunnely of *Shirley*, with its curate Mr. Sweeting.

Gawthorpe Hall, an Elizabethan mansion near Burnley, across the county border from Haworth, in Lancashire. This was the main residence of Sir James and Lady Kay-Shuttleworth who insisted that Charlotte visit them there.

The avenue leading to Gawthorpe Hall.

she stayed with the Kay-Shuttleworths at their Lakeland home and there met Mrs. Gaskell, who became a close friend and later her biographer. The Gaskell's home in Manchester was another place she visited as a guest.

Shy and serious, Charlotte did not glitter in literary society, though she did enjoy her visits to London. She became close to George Smith; some thought that they might marry but years later Smith said:

'No, I never was in the least in love with Charlotte Brontë ... I never was coxcomb enough to suppose that she was in love with

me. But I believe that my mother was at one time rather alarmed.'

James Taylor, a member of his publishing staff, clearly did intend to make a proposal when he came up to Haworth in 1851, prior to his departure as the firm's representative to India. Mr. Brontë liked him and would have approved the match. But Charlotte's 'veins ran ice' at the very thought.

Smith, Elder still declined to publish *The Professor* and Charlotte began work on a story drawing on her experiences in Brussels: *Villette*. The writing did not go smoothly. In the autumn she developed a liver infection made worse by side-effects from the mercury treatment prescribed to treat it. The book was not completed until November 1852. To her distress, the publishers responded to the manuscript with a bank bill for £20, with no covering letter. She was ready to rush up to London to demand an explanation when another letter arrived next day.

Her publishers had not had a new book from her for some time to maintain their interest, and they possibly found this manuscript initially disappointing. A writer was of commercial interest to them first and foremost. It is likely that there were other reasons why their interest had begun to wane. With the solicitous Taylor now in India, the parcels of books became less regular and appeared to have been selected with less care. George Smith had fallen in love with a girl met at a ball and was now married. Smith was quite probably nettled by characters in *Villette* which appeared to have been based upon himself and his mother and by Charlotte's refusal to amend the ending of the story.

At Haworth, Charlotte had another persistent and devoted admirer. Some years before, Charlotte had assured Ellen Nussey that there was no foundation to the rumour of an attachment between her and her father's curate. She had declared that: 'a cold faraway sort of civility are the only terms on which I have ever been with Mr. Nicholls.' But over the years Nicholls must have detected some change of heart, for in December 1852, Charlotte told Ellen Nussey:

'After tea I withdrew from the dining-room as usual ... Mr. Nicholls sat with Papa till between eight and nine o'clock, I then heard him open the parlour door as if going. I expected the clash of the front door. He stopped in the passage: he tapped: like lightning it flashed on me what was coming. He entered – he stood before me. What his words were you can guess; his manner – you can hardly realize – never can I forget it. Shaking from head to foot, looking deadly pale, speaking low, vehemently yet with difficulty – he made me for the first time feel what it costs a man to declare affection where he doubts response.

'The spectacle of one ordinarily so statue-like, thus trembling, stirred, and overcome, gave me a kind of strange shock. He spoke of sufferings he had borne for months, of sufferings he could endure no longer, and craved leave for some hope. I could only entreat him to leave me then and promise a reply on the morrow. I asked if he had spoken to Papa. He said, he dared not. I think I half led, half put him out of the room.'

When he had gone she told her father what had happened. He was furious; he considered it to be an impertinence: the man was below her station, the money she had earned from her book was considerably more than his own income, let alone his curate's, and he needed her presence and support in his old age (he was 75). Charlotte's *'blood boiled with a sense of injustice, but Papa worked himself into a state ... the veins on his temples started up like whipcord, and his eyes became suddenly bloodshot. I made haste to promise that*

Oakwell Hall, the prototype for the home of Shirley Keeldar in Charlotte Brontë's novel, given the name of a neighbouring hamlet: Fieldhead.

'If Fieldhead had few other merits as a building, it might at least be termed picturesque: its irregular architecture, and the grey and mossy colouring communicated by time, gave it a just claim to this epithet. The old latticed windows, the stone porch, the walls, the roof, the chimney-stacks, were rich in crayon touches and sepia lights and shades. The trees behind were fine, bold and spreading; the cedar on the lawn in front was grand, and the granite urns on the garden wall, the fretted arch of the gateway, were, for an artist, as the very desire of the eye.'
Shirley Chapter 11

Mr. Nicholls should on the morrow have a distinct refusal.

'I wrote yesterday and got his note ... Papa's vehement antipathy to the bare thought of me as a wife, and Mr. Nicholl's distress both give me pain. Attachment to Mr. Nicholls ... I never entertained. That he cared something for me, and wanted me to care for him, I have long suspected, but I did not know the degree or strength of his feelings.'

Nicholls resigned his curacy, then withdrew his resignation, but Mr. Brontë would only let him return on a promise that he would never mention marriage again. He was not the only one to have had this strong reaction: sexton John Brown said he would like to shoot Nicholls!

Charlotte went off to London to correct the proofs of *Villette* and for its publication in January 1853. Nicholls agreed to stay until a replacement was found. He thought of emigrating to Australia, and left Haworth in great distress in May, taking with him a gold watch presented by the parishioners. After a short stay in the south of England, he found another Yorkshire curacy near Pontefract. He wrote to Charlotte in the summer and a regular correspondence began. Her father's opposition caused Charlotte to see her suitor in a different light and she was lonely without her brother and sisters. In January 1854, Nicholls made a visit to a friend who was vicar of nearby Oxenhope and the two met often to go walking together. Meanwhile, Mr. Brontë was finding the new curate most unsatisfactory and was beginning to repent the loss of Nicholls. In April, he permitted a visit to the Parsonage, gradually withdrew his opposition to the marriage and, shortly before her 38th birthday, Charlotte became engaged to

The panelling of some rooms at Oakwell Hall was painted white. In *Shirley*, Charlotte Brontë remarks on the drudgery of polishing *'wooden walls with bees-waxed cloths'* and applauds *'the benevolent barbarian who has painted ... the drawing-room ... a delicate pinky white ... enhancing the cheerfulness of his abode, and saving future housemaids a world of toil.'*
Shirley Chapter 7

The Great Hall at Oakwell. As Fieldhead it was *'... Very sombre it was; long, vast, and dark: one latticed window lit it but dimly; the wide old chimney contained now no fire, for the present warm weather needed it not; it was filled instead with willow-boughs. The gallery on high, opposite the entrance, was seen but in outline, so shadowy became this hall towards its ceiling; carved stags' heads, with real antlers, looked down grotesquely from the walls.'*
Shirley Chapter 11

Kirklees Hall and Park, visible from Roe Head, was the model for Nunnwood in *Shirley* (and has also been suggested as an original for Ferndean in *Jane Eyre*).

'On Nunnwood – the sole remnant of antique British forest in a region whose lowlands were once all sylvan chase, as its highlands were breast-deep heather – slept the shadow of a cloud; the distant hills were dappled, the horizon was shaded and tinted like mother-of-pearl; silvery blues, soft purples, evanescent greens and rose-shades, all melting into fleeces of white cloud .... The trees are huge and old. When you stand at their roots, the summits seem in another region, the trunks remain still and firm as pillars, while the boughs sway to every breeze. In the deepest calm their leaves are never quite hushed, and in high wind a flood rushes – a sea thunders above you.'

Shirley Chapter 12

Arthur Bell Nicholls, two years her junior, a serious (if rather narrow-minded) Ulsterman and a graduate of Trinity College, Dublin. She wrote to Ellen Nussey:

'I am engaged ... I am still very calm, very inexpectant. What I taste of happiness is of the soberest order. I trust to love my husband – I am grateful for his tender love to me. I believe him to be an affectionate, a conscientious, a high-principled man; and if, with all this, I should yield to regrets, that fine talents, congenial tastes and thoughts are not added, it seems to me I should be most presumptuous and thankless. Providence offers me this destiny. Doubtless then, it is the best for me.'

This was not the love-match that she would have wanted for one of her own heroines, but nevertheless marriage seems to have brought Charlotte some happiness, if no great passion.

The marriage took place in her father's church on 29 June 1854 with a friend of the groom, the Rev. Sutcliffe Sowden, Vicar of Hebden Bridge, officiating. Miss Wooler and Ellen Nussey were the only guests. The night before, after Mr. Brontë had gone up to bed, he had sent down a message that he would not attend. Whether this was due to the state of his health or sheer cussedness we can only speculate. To replace him, Miss Wooler 'gave away' the bride, for there is no ecclesiastical requirement that this can be only done by a man. A honeymoon in Ireland followed, where Charlotte discovered that her husband's family background was rather more genteel than her own, and on their return they lived at the Parsonage.

Sir James Kay-Shuttleworth offered Nicholls a living at Padiham, but it was felt impossible to leave Mr. Brontë, so it was declined. The new Mrs. Nicholls helped with parish duties and settled

The view from Roe Head. Though industrial sprawl was less, Charlotte Brontë would have been well aware of the mills and factories of the valley. Machine-wrecking Luddites gathered here in April 1812 before attacking Rawfold's Mill two miles away beyond Liversedge and near Cleckheaton. Newspaper reports, and her father's memories of such Luddite action, were used as raw material for *Shirley*.

The Taylors' Hunsworth Mill, downstream from Rawfold's on the Dewsbury Beck, was built in 1785 to process wool and weave and dye woollen cloth. When Charlotte Brontë used it as Hollows Mill in *Shirley*, the valley here below Oakwell Hall and Gomersal was still a wooded ravine with bluebells.

into married life.

At the end of November Charlotte went for a walk on the moors with Arthur and he suggested that they go up South Dean Beck to see the waterfall in spate, for there had been a great fall of snow which was now melting. As they admired it, it began to rain. On the 3-mile-walk home, Charlotte was soaked and developed a persistent cold. She was forced to cancel a planned visit to Ellen Nussey at Brookroyd. Though not fully recovered, it was more difficult for her to turn down an invitation from the Kay-Shuttleworths to visit Gawn-thorpe Hall. Walks in the wet while she was there in the New Year made her condition worse.

By now Charlotte had realized that she was pregnant and the doctor considered the condition to be exacerbating the sickness and ill-health she was now experiencing. Eventually,

she was forced to take to her bed. Despite the dedicated nursing of her husband and Martha Brown, she seemed to be growing increasingly weak. Another, more eminent, doctor was summoned from Bradford. He declared that her condition was not dangerous, though her illness might last for some time.

While Charlotte lay sick, Flossy, Anne's spaniel dog, died quietly one night and then Tabby Aykroyd was taken ill. Tabby was taken to her sister's home where she also died. It must have been difficult to find a ray of hope in the parsonage at that time. On March 30, Mr. Brontë replied to a letter from Ellen Nussey:

'We are in great trouble, and Mr. Nicholls so much so, that he is not sufficiently strong and composed as to be able to write my dear Daughter is very ill, and apparently on the verge of the grave. If she could speak, she would no doubt dictate to us while answering your kind letter, but we are left to give what answer we can. The Doctors have no hope of her case ...'

Charlotte Brontë died in the early hours of the night of 31 March 1855.

The Professor was eventually published in 1857, the same year as Mrs. Gaskell's *The Life of Charlotte Brontë*, written at Mr. Brontë's request. Arthur Nicholls stayed at Haworth until Patrick Brontë's death, aged 85, in 1861. He then returned to Ireland where he later married a cousin and became a farmer. With him, he took the portrait of Charlotte by George Richmond (which he bequeathed to The National Portrait Gallery), her wedding dress, Mr. Brontë's dog Plato, the servant, Martha Brown and various letters and mementoes. These included some of the notes which Emily and Anne were in the habit of writing on their birthdays, to be opened and read four years later, and some of the little books in microscopic handwriting which the Brontës had written in their childhood. They were discovered among his belongings after his death in 1906.